AF492082

# Beneath the Waves: Navigators' Nightmares and Modern Piracy Along the Coasts of Somalia

ROBERTO MIGUEL RODRIGUEZ

2023

Copyright Page

TITLE: Beneath the Waves: Navigators' Nightmares and Modern Piracy Along the Coasts of Somalia

1<sup>ST</sup> Edition

Copyright @ 2023

Roberto M. Rodriguez. All rights reserved.

ISBN: 9798223806400

# Table of Contents

Beneath the Waves: Navigators' Nightmares and Modern Piracy Along the Coasts of Somalia

By Roberto Miguel Rodriguez

# Chapter 1: Navigators' Nightmares: Modern Piracy Along the Coasts of Somalia

The History and Evolution of Piracy in the Region

Piracy has plagued the region's waters throughout history, creating nightmares for navigators and seafarers alike. From its early beginnings to the modern era, piracy has evolved and adapted, presenting unique challenges for historians, diplomats, navigators, and maritime operators to understand and combat.

The roots of piracy in the region can be traced back centuries, with the notorious Barbary pirates dominating the seas during the 16th and 17th centuries. These pirates, hailing from the North African coast, terrorized European ships, capturing their cargo and enslaving their crews. Their actions threatened maritime trade and strained diplomatic relations between nations.

However, in the late 20th century, piracy in the region took a new and alarming turn. The failed state of Somalia and its vast coastline presented the perfect breeding ground for modern piracy. As the country descended into chaos, armed militias took to the sea, hijacking ships and demanding hefty ransoms. This marked a significant shift from the traditional piracy model, where pirates sought to capture goods rather than hostages.

In response to this emerging threat, international naval forces launched counter-piracy efforts, patrolling the waters off the coast of Somalia and establishing a strong presence to deter pirate attacks. Although successful in reducing piracy incidents, these efforts have not entirely eradicated the problem.

The psychological impact on seafarers and navigators cannot be underestimated. The constant fear of pirate attacks and the trauma associated with being held hostage leave a lasting impact on those who fall victim to piracy. Navigators' nightmares are real and can affect their ability to perform their duties effectively and confidently.

The economic implications of piracy on maritime trade are vast. Insurance premiums skyrocket, shipping routes are altered to avoid high-risk areas, and the cost of piracy-related security measures burdens the industry. The legal challenges in prosecuting pirates are also complex, with jurisdictional issues and the difficulty of gathering evidence often hampering efforts to bring pirates to justice.

Private security firms have emerged as key players in protecting ships against pirate attacks. These firms employ armed guards and use advanced technology to deter and defend against pirate threats. However, their role is not without controversy, as questions of legality and the potential for escalation of violence arise.

The impact of piracy extends beyond the maritime industry. Local communities and economies in Somalia have been profoundly affected, with pirates often reinvesting their ransom money into their communities. This has created a complex web of conspiracy and dependency that is challenging to unravel.

Technological advancements have played a crucial role in enhancing maritime security against piracy. From satellite surveillance to developing early warning systems, these advancements have helped detect and prevent pirate attacks, providing navigators and maritime operators a valuable tool in their battle against piracy.

Strategies for preventing and responding to pirate attacks continue to evolve. From increased cooperation between naval forces and shipping companies to establishing safe corridors and using armed guards, a multi-faceted approach is necessary to combat piracy in the region effectively.

Lastly, the environmental consequences of piracy in Somali waters cannot be ignored. Illegal fishing and the dumping of toxic waste by pirate groups have devastated marine ecosystems, further exacerbating the challenges faced by the region.

The history and evolution of piracy in the region provide valuable insights into the complex nature of this maritime threat. By understanding its origins and adapting to its changing tactics, historians, diplomats, navigators, and maritime operators can work together to find innovative solutions to combat piracy and ensure the safety of seafarers and the integrity of maritime trade.

Psychological Impact on Seafarers and Navigators

The treacherous waters off the coasts of Somalia have long been a nightmare for navigators, haunted by the ever-present threat of modern piracy. While the focus of discussions about piracy often revolves around economic implications, legal challenges, and counter-piracy efforts, it is crucial to shed light on the profound psychological impact these harrowing experiences have on seafarers and navigators.

Navigating through pirate-infested waters is a mentally and emotionally taxing task. The constant fear of an attack, the uncertainty of the situation, and the knowledge that one wrong move could lead to disaster create a sense of constant vigilance and heightened anxiety. Sleep deprivation becomes a norm as navigators and seafarers must remain vigilant to protect themselves and their vessels.

The psychological toll is further exacerbated by the trauma of witnessing acts of violence and brutality. Pirates often resort to extreme measures, including physical assault, kidnapping, and murder. These traumatizing experiences can leave seafarers and navigators plagued by nightmares, post-traumatic stress disorder (PTSD), and other mental health issues.

The impact is not limited to individuals alone; it affects the entire crew and maritime operations' overall safety and efficiency. Crew members dealing with psychological distress may struggle to concentrate, make sound decisions, or effectively communicate, jeopardizing the safety of the entire vessel. The long-lasting effects of psychological trauma can also lead to higher turnover rates among seafarers, impacting the stability of the maritime workforce.

Recognizing the significance of addressing the psychological impact on seafarers and navigators, efforts have been made to provide support and resources. Maritime operators have implemented psychological support programs, training crews to recognize signs of distress and providing access to counseling services. Additionally, cooperation between naval forces and private security firms has improved protection measures and a more secure environment, alleviating some psychological burdens on seafarers and navigators.

Understanding the psychological impact of piracy is vital not only for the well-being of seafarers and navigators but also for the success of counter-piracy efforts. By prioritizing the mental health of those who brave the treacherous waters, we can ensure safer maritime operations and contribute to the overall stability and security of the region.

As historians, diplomats, navigators, and maritime operators, it is essential to consider piracy's psychological toll on those who dare to navigate these dangerous waters. By shedding light on this often overlooked aspect, we can work towards comprehensive solutions that address seafarers' and navigators' physical and psychological well-being, creating a safer and more sustainable maritime environment.

Economic Implications of Piracy on Maritime Trade

Piracy along the coasts of Somalia has had significant economic implications on maritime trade, affecting not only local communities and economies but also international stakeholders. This subchapter explores the intricate relationship between piracy and the global economy, shedding light on the various aspects affected by this modern-day maritime menace.

One of the most apparent economic impacts of piracy is increased shipping costs. As vessels passing through the Somali waters face the risk of pirate attacks, shipping companies must take precautionary measures to safeguard their cargo and crew. This often involves rerouting ships, increasing security measures, and deploying private security firms. These additional expenses are ultimately passed on to consumers, leading to higher prices for goods transported through these routes.

Moreover, the threat of piracy has led to a decline in trade volumes in the affected regions. Fearing attacks and potential losses, shipping companies opt for alternative routes, bypassing Somali waters altogether. This redirection of trade disrupts established supply chains and trading patterns, causing economic losses for countries relying on maritime trade with Somalia and its neighbouring regions.

The local economies in Somalia have also been profoundly affected by piracy. The lawless activities have hindered the development of the fishing industry, which was once a vital source of income for coastal communities. With the fear of pirate attacks, many fishermen have been deterred from venturing into the sea, leading to a decline in seafood exports and a loss of livelihood for thousands of people.

Furthermore, piracy has undermined foreign direct investment in the region. Investors are reluctant to engage in economic ventures in areas plagued by piracy, fearing the safety of their assets and personnel. This lack of investment hampers economic development and perpetuates Somalia's poverty cycle.

In conclusion, piracy along the coasts of Somalia has far-reaching economic implications for maritime trade. It increases shipping costs, disrupts trade volumes, hampers local economies, and deters foreign investment. Addressing the economic consequences of piracy requires a comprehensive approach involving international cooperation, effective counter-piracy efforts, and the implementation of strategies to mitigate the risks faced by the maritime industry. We can work towards a sustainable solution to this navigators' nightmare by understanding and addressing the economic impacts.

Environmental Consequences of Piracy in Somali Waters

Piracy in Somali waters has not only had profound social, economic, and political implications but has also inflicted severe environmental consequences. The subchapter "Environmental Consequences of Piracy in Somali Waters" delves into the often-overlooked ecological impacts of piracy in this region. This section of the book "Beneath the Waves: Navigators' Nightmares and Modern Piracy Along the Coasts of Somalia" is essential for historians, diplomats, navigators, and maritime operators seeking a comprehensive understanding of the multifaceted nature of piracy.

The Somali coastline is home to diverse marine ecosystems, including coral reefs, seagrass meadows, and mangroves. However, the activities of pirates have significantly disrupted these delicate habitats. One of the most immediate and visible impacts is pirate gangs' illegal dumping of toxic waste. Taking advantage of the lawlessness in the region, evil corporations and criminal syndicates have used Somali waters as a dumping ground for hazardous materials. These pollutants pose a direct threat to marine life and have long-term consequences for the health of local communities dependent on fishing and tourism.

Moreover, the hijacking of vessels and the subsequent holding of crew members hostage have led to releasing oil and other hazardous substances into the marine environment. The accidental spills during pirate attacks or the deliberate discharge by pirates seeking to evade naval forces have resulted in oil slicks, contaminating coastlines and devastating marine life. The impact on fisheries, a lifeline for many coastal communities, has been particularly severe, with a decline in fish stocks, loss of livelihoods, and food insecurity.

In addition to direct pollution, piracy has indirectly contributed to environmental degradation. The increased naval presence in Somali waters to combat piracy has led to a surge in shipping traffic, resulting in ship strikes on marine mammals and collisions with coral reefs. This has further disrupted the delicate balance of these ecosystems and exacerbated the decline of endangered species.

Understanding the environmental consequences of piracy in Somali waters is crucial for developing effective counter-piracy strategies. Policymakers, naval forces, and maritime operators must consider the ecological implications when formulating plans to combat piracy. Collaboration between international organizations, governments, and local communities is essential to address these environmental challenges and restore the marine ecosystems of this region.

In conclusion, the subchapter on "Environmental Consequences of Piracy in Somali Waters" sheds light on the often-neglected ecological impacts of piracy. By exploring the illegal dumping of toxic waste, oil spills, disruptions to marine ecosystems, and the indirect consequences of increased maritime traffic, this section provides a comprehensive understanding of the environmental devastation caused by piracy. This knowledge is vital for historians, diplomats, navigators, and maritime operators seeking a holistic perspective on the multifaceted nature of piracy in Somali waters and the urgent need for sustainable solutions.

# Chapter 2: Counter-piracy Efforts by International Naval Forces

Strategies for Preventing and Responding to Pirate Attacks

In the treacherous waters along the coasts of Somalia, pirate attacks have become a pressing concern for historians, diplomats, navigators, and maritime operators alike. To combat this modern-day scourge, a comprehensive set of strategies must be implemented to effectively prevent and respond to pirate attacks.

Prevention is key in the battle against piracy. One of the most effective strategies is establishing a robust international naval presence in the region. By coordinating efforts and patrolling the waters, naval forces can deter pirates and swiftly respond to threats. This collaboration among nations has proven successful in mitigating pirate attacks, as demonstrated by the counter-piracy efforts witnessed over the years.

Additionally, deploying private security firms onboard ships has proven an effective preventive measure. These firms provide armed guards with the expertise to repel pirate attacks. Their presence is a powerful deterrent, discouraging pirates from targeting vulnerable vessels.

Furthermore, technological advancements in maritime security are crucial in preventing pirate attacks. Enhanced radar systems, high-tech surveillance equipment, and real-time communication systems enable swift identification and response to potential threats. Investing in these technologies is essential to ensure seafarers' safety and protect valuable cargo.

However, despite preventative measures, pirate attacks may still occur. Responding effectively to such incidents is equally important. Prompt reporting of attacks to naval forces and coordination among ships in the area can lead to a rapid response, increasing the chances of successfully apprehending pirates and rescuing hostages.

Legal challenges in prosecuting pirates must also be addressed. International collaboration is necessary to ensure that captured pirates are brought to justice and face appropriate legal consequences for their actions. Cooperation between nations is crucial to establish a framework for prosecuting and convicting pirates and deterring others from piracy.

Finally, it is essential to recognize the psychological impact on seafarers and navigators who have experienced pirate attacks. Proper support systems and counseling services should be provided to help them cope with trauma and facilitate their reintegration into maritime operations.

By implementing these strategies, historians, diplomats, navigators, and maritime operators can work together to combat piracy along the coasts of Somalia. Not only will these efforts protect lives and cargo, but they will also contribute to the stability and economic prosperity of the region.

Technological Advancements in Maritime Security Against Piracy

Maritime security has become an increasingly critical concern in recent years, particularly in regions such as the coasts of Somalia, which have witnessed a surge in modern piracy. This subchapter explores the technological advancements developed to combat piracy and protect seafarers, vessels, and trade routes.

The advent of technology has revolutionized how maritime security is approached. Historically, the response to piracy relied heavily on the presence of naval forces, but today, technological innovations play a pivotal role in deterring and responding to pirate attacks.

One such advancement is the use of satellite technology. Satellites equipped with high-resolution cameras and radar systems provide real-time surveillance and monitoring of maritime activities. These satellites can detect suspicious vessels, track their movements, and provide crucial information to naval forces, enabling them to respond swiftly and effectively. Additionally, satellite communication systems have improved the ability to relay information between ships and coastal authorities, promoting rapid response times and coordinated efforts.

Unmanned Aerial Vehicles (UAVs), commonly known as drones, have also emerged as a valuable tool in maritime security. Equipped with thermal imaging cameras and advanced sensors, drones can patrol vast areas of the ocean, providing an aerial perspective that was previously unattainable. Their ability to gather intelligence, detect potential threats, and conduct surveillance makes them an invaluable asset in combating piracy.

Furthermore, advancements in sensor technology have led to the development of sophisticated underwater detection systems. These systems employ sonar and acoustic sensors to detect and track underwater threats, such as submarines or small boats used by pirates. By providing early warnings, these systems allow naval forces to take preemptive action and prevent pirate attacks.

In recent years, non-lethal deterrents have gained momentum as an effective strategy against piracy. Acoustic devices, known as Long Range Acoustic Devices (LRADs), emit high-intensity sound waves that can disorient and deter pirates. Similarly, water cannons and laser dazzlers deter approaching vessels without causing harm.

Integrating these technological advancements into a comprehensive maritime security framework has significantly improved the ability to prevent, detect, and respond to pirate attacks. However, it is important to adapt and innovate as pirates also evolve their tactics continually. Regular updates in technology, training, and collaboration between naval forces, private security firms, and maritime operators are crucial in ensuring the safety of seafarers and the protection of maritime trade routes against modern piracy threats.

The Role of Private Security Firms in Protecting Ships

In recent years, the threat of piracy along the coasts of Somalia has become a significant concern for historians, diplomats, navigators, and maritime operators. As the number of pirate attacks continues to rise, exploring various strategies for countering this menace has become essential. One such approach is the involvement of private security firms in protecting ships navigating these treacherous waters.

Private security firms play a crucial role in safeguarding vessels from pirate attacks. They provide a range of services, including armed guards, security assessments, and consultancy, which help mitigate the risks associated with piracy. Armed guards on board are a deterrent, making it less likely for pirates to target a vessel. These guards are highly trained and equipped to handle any potential threat, ensuring the safety of the crew and cargo.

Moreover, private security firms conduct comprehensive security assessments to identify vulnerabilities and develop tailored strategies for each ship. These assessments include evaluating the vessel's route, analyzing historical pirate activity, and recommending appropriate security measures. By implementing these measures, ships can significantly reduce the likelihood of pirate attacks and increase their overall security.

The involvement of private security firms also addresses the psychological impact of piracy on seafarers and navigators. Knowing that professionals protect their ships provides security and peace of mind, allowing crew members to focus on their duties without constantly fearing for their lives. This psychological well-being is crucial in ensuring the efficient operation of the vessel and the safety of all on board.

From an economic perspective, piracy has severe implications for maritime trade. The hijacking of ships and the subsequent payment of ransoms resulted in excessive financial losses. Private security firms help mitigate these economic implications by minimizing the risk of attacks and reducing the need for ransom payments. By protecting ships, these firms contribute to the region's stability and profitability of maritime trade routes.

However, the involvement of private security firms also raises legal challenges in prosecuting pirates. Using armed guards and the potential for lethal force in self-defense requires careful legal considerations. International laws and regulations must be developed and implemented to ensure private security firms operate within a legal framework while effectively protecting ships.

In conclusion, private security firms play a vital role in protecting ships navigating the coasts of Somalia. Their services act as a deterrent, provide security assessments, address the psychological impact on seafarers, mitigate economic implications, and address legal challenges. By collaborating with international naval forces and other stakeholders, private security firms contribute to the overall strategy for countering piracy and ensuring the safety of maritime operations in the region.

# Chapter 3: Legal Challenges in Prosecuting Pirates

International Laws and Conventions About Maritime Piracy

Maritime piracy has been a persistent threat along the coasts of Somalia, causing significant challenges for navigators, maritime operators, and the international community. To address this issue effectively, it is crucial to understand the international laws and conventions that govern maritime piracy and guide counter-piracy efforts.

One of the key legal instruments in combating piracy is the United Nations Convention on the Law of the Sea (UNCLOS). UNCLOS provides a comprehensive framework for the rights and responsibilities of states regarding maritime piracy. It establishes the jurisdiction of states over acts of piracy committed on the high seas and addresses the prosecution, extradition, and punishment of pirates.

Additionally, several regional and international agreements have been established to enhance cooperation and coordination among nations in combating piracy. Notably, the Djibouti Code of Conduct and the Regional Cooperation Agreement on Combating Piracy and Armed Robbery against Ships in Asia (ReCAAP) are essential in facilitating information sharing, capacity building, and joint naval patrols.

The international naval forces have played a crucial role in deterring and suppressing piracy off the coast of Somalia. The European Union Naval Force Somalia (EU NAVFOR), NATO's Operation Ocean Shield, and the Combined Maritime Forces (CMF) have been actively patrolling and escorting merchant vessels, conducting surveillance, and apprehending pirates. These initiatives have significantly contributed to reducing pirate attacks and ensuring the safety of seafarers.

However, it is important to recognize that piracy poses physical threats and has severe psychological impacts on seafarers and navigators. The trauma experienced by those subjected to piracy can have long-lasting effects on their mental well-being. Efforts must be made to ensure proper psychological support and counseling for affected individuals.

Moreover, piracy has far-reaching economic implications for maritime trade. The cost of increased insurance premiums, vessel rerouting, and hiring private security firms for protection significantly affects the profitability of maritime operations. Additionally, piracy disrupts the flow of goods and increases consumer prices, particularly in the affected regions.

Prosecuting pirates pose significant legal challenges due to jurisdictional issues and the need to gather evidence from international waters. The international community must work together to strengthen legal frameworks and improve coordination to ensure effective prosecution of pirates.

Private security firms have emerged as crucial in protecting ships from pirate attacks. These firms employ various measures such as armed guards, secure citadels, and technological advancements to deter and repel pirates. However, concerns regarding the use of force and the potential for escalation must be carefully managed.

The impact of piracy extends beyond the shipping industry and affects local communities and economies in Somalia. Piracy has served as a source of income for many individuals left with limited alternatives due to political instability and economic hardships. Addressing local grievances and providing sustainable livelihoods are essential in eradicating piracy from the region.

Technological advancements in maritime security, such as improved surveillance systems, early warning mechanisms, and the use of drones, have proven effective in preventing pirate attacks. These advancements must be further developed and deployed to enhance the safety and security of maritime operations.

Strategies for preventing and responding to pirate attacks require a comprehensive approach, including intelligence sharing, capacity building, and establishing secure transit corridors. Collaboration between governments, international organizations, and maritime industry stakeholders is crucial in implementing effective counter-piracy measures.

Lastly, the environmental consequences of piracy in Somali waters cannot be ignored. Pollution from hijacked vessels, illegal fishing, and toxic waste dumping negatively impact marine ecosystems and the livelihoods of local communities. Efforts must be made to address these environmental challenges in conjunction with counter-piracy efforts.

Understanding the history and evolution of piracy in the region provides valuable insights into the root causes and underlying factors that contribute to its persistence. By examining historical precedents and the changing dynamics of piracy, policymakers, historians, and diplomats can develop informed strategies to tackle this enduring problem effectively.

In conclusion, international laws and conventions about maritime piracy provide a crucial framework for addressing this complex issue. Efforts to combat piracy must encompass legal, operational, and socio-economic dimensions while considering the specific challenges navigators, maritime operators, and local communities face. By employing a comprehensive approach, the international community can effectively deter, suppress, and ultimately eradicate piracy from the coasts of Somalia.

Challenges in Gathering Sufficient Evidence and Jurisdiction Issues

When combating modern piracy along the coasts of Somalia, one of the most significant challenges faced by international naval forces, historians, diplomats, navigators, and maritime operators is gathering sufficient evidence to prosecute pirates. This subchapter delves into the various hurdles faced in this aspect and jurisdiction issues that further complicate the process.

The first challenge lies in the vastness of the maritime domain. The Somali waters stretch over thousands of miles, making monitoring and gathering evidence of pirate activities difficult. Navigators and maritime operators often navigate treacherous waters, increasing the risk of encounters with pirates. The sheer expanse of the area makes it arduous to collect concrete evidence, as pirates can easily blend into the vastness of the sea.

Additionally, pirates have become increasingly sophisticated, employing tactics such as mother ships and hijacked fishing vessels to extend their reach. This further complicates evidence gathering as distinguishing between pirates and innocent fishermen becomes challenging. It requires a deep understanding of the region's dynamics and a comprehensive intelligence network to distinguish between them.

Jurisdiction issues pose another significant challenge in prosecuting pirates. Somalia has been plagued by political instability and lacks a functioning central government. This creates a legal vacuum, making establishing jurisdiction over captured pirates difficult. Historians, diplomats, and legal experts face the complex task of navigating through a web of legal frameworks to determine the most suitable jurisdiction for prosecution.

Furthermore, the involvement of private security firms in protecting ships adds another layer of complexity. The legal status and authority of these private entities often become blurred, raising questions about the admissibility of evidence collected by them. This challenge highlights the need for clear legal guidelines and cooperation between naval forces, private security firms, and local authorities to ensure a seamless prosecution process.

In conclusion, gathering sufficient evidence and addressing jurisdiction issues are daunting challenges in the fight against piracy along the coasts of Somalia. Navigators, maritime operators, historians, and diplomats must work collaboratively to overcome these hurdles. By employing advanced technological advancements, establishing clear legal frameworks, and fostering international cooperation, stakeholders can enhance their efforts to combat piracy effectively. Only through a comprehensive approach can we hope to end the navigators' nightmares and protect the seas from the scourge of modern piracy.

Cooperation and Coordination Amongst Nations in Prosecuting Pirates

The fight against piracy along the coasts of Somalia has been long and arduous. It is a battle that has required nations' collective efforts to bring these criminals to justice. Cooperation and coordination amongst nations in prosecuting pirates have played a crucial role in combating this modern-day scourge of the seas.

Historians, diplomats, navigators, and maritime operators have witnessed firsthand the devastating impact of piracy on the region. The subchapter "Cooperation and Coordination Amongst Nations in Prosecuting Pirates" explores the collaborative efforts undertaken to tackle this issue.

Counter-piracy efforts by international naval forces have deterred and apprehended pirates. The coordination between nations, through joint patrols and information sharing, has allowed for a more effective response to pirate attacks. This has protected seafarers and navigators and ensured the safe passage of maritime trade.

However, the fight against piracy is not just a physical battle; it also has psychological and economic implications. Seafarers and navigators have faced immense psychological trauma due to pirate attacks. The subchapter delves into the psychological impact on these individuals and explores measures that can be taken to support their well-being.

Furthermore, the economic consequences of piracy on maritime trade cannot be ignored. The subchapter examines the ripple effect of piracy, from increased insurance costs to disrupted supply chains. It also highlights the legal challenges in prosecuting pirates and the need for international cooperation to ensure justice.

Private security firms have also played a critical role in protecting ships from pirate attacks. The subchapter explores their involvement and the effectiveness of their strategies in safeguarding vessels and their crew.

Moreover, the impact of piracy on local communities and economies in Somalia cannot be overlooked. The subchapter sheds light on the socio-economic consequences faced by these communities and the need for holistic approaches to address the root causes of piracy.

Technological advancements in maritime security have also played a significant role in combating piracy. From improved surveillance systems to using drones, these advancements have enhanced the ability to detect and respond to pirate activities.

In conclusion, the subchapter "Cooperation and Coordination Amongst Nations in Prosecuting Pirates" highlights the collective efforts required to combat piracy along the coasts of Somalia. It addresses the various aspects of this issue, including the historical context, counter-piracy efforts, psychological impact, economic implications, legal challenges, private security involvement, and technological advancements. By understanding the multifaceted nature of piracy, we can work towards developing effective strategies for preventing and responding to pirate attacks while also addressing the environmental consequences and the historical evolution of piracy in the region.

# Chapter 4: Impact of Piracy on Local Communities and Economies in Somalia

Socioeconomic Consequences on Coastal Communities

The issue of piracy along the coasts of Somalia has had far-reaching consequences for the socioeconomic fabric of the region's coastal communities. This subchapter aims to shed light on the impact of piracy on these communities, focusing on the economic and social implications that have resulted from the rise of modern piracy.

The coastal communities of Somalia have historically relied heavily on maritime trade as a livelihood. The rise of piracy has disrupted this trade, leading to a significant decline in economic activity and increased poverty levels. With pirate attacks becoming more frequent and violent, many seafarers and navigators are deterred from entering Somali waters, diverting their routes and trade to alternative ports. This has resulted in a loss of revenue for the coastal communities, as well as a decline in employment opportunities in the maritime sector.

Furthermore, piracy has also had a detrimental effect on the local economies. The fear of pirate attacks has discouraged foreign investment and trade partnerships, hindering the growth of industries such as fishing and tourism, which are vital for developing coastal communities. Additionally, the communities have faced challenges in attracting international aid and assistance due to the insecurity caused by piracy, further exacerbating the dire socioeconomic conditions.

The consequences of piracy extend beyond the economic realm and have deeply impacted the social fabric of these communities. The constant threat of violence and kidnapping has created fear and trauma among the residents. Seafarers and navigators who have fallen victim to pirate attacks often have post-traumatic stress disorder (PTSD) and other psychological disorders, affecting their ability to work and support their families. Moreover, the disruption of trade and the resulting poverty have contributed to social unrest, leading to increased crime rates and the rise of piracy as a means of survival for some individuals.

In conclusion, the socioeconomic consequences of piracy on the coastal communities of Somalia have been severe. The decline in economic activity, loss of employment, and the disruption of trade have plunged these communities into poverty and instability. Additionally, the psychological impact on seafarers and navigators further compounds these communities' challenges. Addressing this issue requires comprehensive strategies that focus on maritime security and prioritize the economic development and social well-being of the affected communities.

Influence on Livelihoods and Fishing Industries

The impact of piracy along the coasts of Somalia goes beyond the immediate threat to seafarers and navigators. One of the most affected sectors is the fishing industry, which pirates in the region have severely disrupted. This subchapter delves into the influence of piracy on livelihoods and fishing industries, shedding light on the consequences faced by local communities and economies in Somalia.

Historically, Somalia's waters have been rich in marine resources, providing a source of income for thousands of fishermen and their families. However, the rise of modern piracy has drastically changed the dynamics of the fishing industry. Fishermen now face constant fear and danger while trying to make a living. The risk of being attacked, kidnapped, or having their vessels hijacked has forced many fishermen to abandon their livelihoods, leaving their communities struggling to make ends meet.

Moreover, the economic implications of piracy on maritime trade have further exacerbated the already dire situation. With piracy disrupting shipping routes and increasing insurance costs, many international companies have avoided the Somali waters altogether. This has significantly declined trade and economic activity in the region, negatively impacting the already fragile local economies.

The legal challenges in prosecuting pirates have also hindered efforts to combat piracy effectively. The complex jurisdictional issues, lack of evidence, and difficulties in apprehending pirates have made it challenging to bring them to justice. Additionally, the role of private security firms in protecting ships has raised ethical concerns, as their presence and actions have sometimes escalated tensions and contributed to the cycle of violence.

Various counter-piracy efforts have been implemented to address these challenges, including technological advancements in maritime security. Improved surveillance systems, enhanced communication networks, and the deployment of international naval forces have all played a crucial role in deterring pirate attacks. However, the effectiveness of these measures is still debated, and further strategies for preventing and responding to pirate attacks need to be explored.

The consequences of piracy extend beyond the human and economic spheres. The environmental impact of piracy in Somali waters is another pressing concern. The illegal dumping of toxic waste by pirate vessels and the destruction of coral reefs and marine habitats during attacks have had long-lasting consequences for the fragile marine ecosystem.

Understanding the influence of piracy on livelihoods and fishing industries is vital for historians, diplomats, navigators, and maritime operators. It highlights the interconnectedness of various piracy-related aspects, including the economic, legal, psychological, and environmental dimensions. By comprehending these influences, stakeholders can collaborate more effectively to develop comprehensive strategies that address the root causes of piracy and promote sustainable maritime security in the region.

Efforts to Alleviate Poverty and Promote Development

In the face of the daunting challenges posed by modern piracy along the coasts of Somalia, the international community has recognized the need for comprehensive efforts to alleviate poverty and promote development in the region. Historians, diplomats, navigators, and maritime operators have all played crucial roles in understanding the socio-economic factors contributing to piracy and formulating strategies to address them.

The roots of piracy in Somalia can be traced back to the collapse of the central government in 1991, which resulted in widespread lawlessness and economic instability. As a result, poverty levels soared, and coastal communities turned to piracy to survive. To tackle this issue, various initiatives have been undertaken to address the underlying causes of poverty and promote sustainable development.

One such effort is the establishment of international naval forces to combat piracy. These forces, composed of vessels from different nations, have been deployed to patrol the waters off the Somali coast, deter pirate attacks, and ensure the safety of seafarers and navigators. This coordinated approach has significantly reduced the number of successful pirate attacks in recent years.

However, it is essential to recognize the psychological impact that piracy has had on seafarers and navigators. The constant fear of being attacked and held hostage has affected their mental health. To address this issue, support and counseling services have been provided to those affected, helping them cope with the trauma and enabling them to continue their vital work.

The economic implications of piracy on maritime trade cannot be ignored either. The high cost of piracy, including ransom payments, increased insurance premiums, and vessel rerouting, has affected global trade. Efforts have been made to enhance security measures, such as deploying private security firms to protect ships and deter pirate attacks.

Moreover, the impact of piracy extends beyond the maritime sector. Local communities in Somalia have suffered greatly from the presence of pirates, who disrupt fishing activities and extort money from coastal populations. To counter this, development projects have been implemented to provide alternative livelihoods, such as vocational training and job creation, reducing the incentives for individuals to engage in piracy.

Technological advancements have also played a vital role in enhancing maritime security against piracy. Surveillance systems, such as radar and satellite tracking, have been utilized to detect and monitor pirate activities, allowing for timely intervention by naval forces. Additionally, strategies for preventing and responding to pirate attacks have been developed, including establishing safe corridors and strengthening legal frameworks for prosecuting pirates.

The environmental consequences of piracy in Somali waters cannot be overlooked either. Illegal fishing, toxic waste dumping, and pirate oil smuggling have significantly damaged marine ecosystems. Efforts have been made to address these environmental challenges, including increased monitoring and cooperation between international organizations to protect the fragile marine environment.

Understanding the history and evolution of piracy in the region is crucial for devising effective long-term solutions. By examining the root causes and historical context, policymakers can develop targeted interventions that address the underlying socio-economic issues and contribute to the sustainable development of Somalia.

In conclusion, efforts to alleviate poverty and promote development are essential in addressing the challenges posed by modern piracy along the coasts of Somalia. Historians, diplomats, navigators, and maritime operators have all played significant roles in understanding the issue's complexities and formulating strategies to combat piracy. The international community can strive towards a future free from piracy and its associated socio-economic consequences by addressing poverty, enhancing maritime security, supporting affected individuals, and implementing sustainable development projects.

# Chapter 5: The Role of Private Security Firms in Protecting Ships

Private Security Firms: Services and Advantages

In the treacherous waters off the coasts of Somalia, where modern piracy has reached alarming heights, the role of private security firms in protecting ships has become indispensable. These firms offer a range of services and advantages that have proven effective in countering pirate attacks, ensuring the safety of seafarers and preserving the integrity of maritime trade.

Private security firms provide a comprehensive security package for ships operating in piracy-infested waters. Their services include deploying armed security teams, who are highly trained and experienced in dealing with hostile situations at sea. These teams act as a strong deterrent to pirates, significantly reducing the risk of attacks. Additionally, they employ advanced surveillance and monitoring systems to detect and track potential pirate threats, enabling early intervention and proactive measures to prevent attacks.

One of the greatest advantages of hiring private security firms is their ability to adapt and respond quickly to evolving pirate tactics. These firms constantly analyze and assess the changing modus operandi of pirates, ensuring that their strategies remain effective. They employ passive and active defense measures, such as razor wire, electrified fences, and non-lethal weapons, to protect ships and their crew. This versatility and adaptability are crucial in staying one step ahead of the pirates and maintaining a safe operating environment.

Private security firms also have a significant psychological impact on seafarers and navigators. Knowing that a professional security team protects their ship instils a sense of confidence and peace of mind among the crew. This, in turn, enhances their morale and overall well-being, enabling them to perform their duties more effectively. Reducing stress and anxiety associated with pirate attacks also has long-term psychological benefits, minimizing the risk of post-traumatic stress disorder (PTSD) and other mental health issues among seafarers.

From an economic perspective, the services provided by private security firms are invaluable. Piracy poses a grave threat to maritime trade, leading to increased insurance premiums, ship rerouting, and cargo delivery delays. Private security firms help mitigate these economic implications by preventing pirate attacks, enabling smooth and uninterrupted trade. The cost of hiring security teams outweighs the potential losses and damages that piracy can inflict on ships and their cargo.

In conclusion, private security firms play a crucial role in safeguarding ships and countering piracy along the coasts of Somalia. Their services and advantages, including armed security teams, advanced surveillance systems, adaptability, psychological impact, and economic benefits, make them an indispensable asset in protecting seafarers, preserving maritime trade, and ensuring the safety and security of ships in these dangerous waters.

Challenges and Controversies Surrounding the Use of Private Security

Private security firms have emerged as a critical component in protecting ships from pirate attacks along the coasts of Somalia. However, their involvement has not been without challenges and controversies. This subchapter explores the various issues surrounding the use of private security in the fight against piracy.

One of the primary challenges is the legal framework surrounding the use of private security firms. While their services are in high demand, the legal challenges in prosecuting pirates often extend to private security personnel. The lines between self-defence and vigilantism can become blurred, raising questions about the legitimacy of their actions. As a result, there is a need for clear guidelines and regulations to ensure that private security firms operate within the boundaries of the law.

Another controversy stems from the economic implications of piracy on maritime trade. Private security firms are often contracted by ship owners, leading to additional costs that can burden the already struggling maritime industry. There are debates about who should bear the financial responsibility for protecting ships, with some arguing for international cooperation to fund the security measures.

Furthermore, the impact of private security on local communities and economies in Somalia is a subject of concern. While their presence can deter pirate attacks, it can also exacerbate regional tensions and conflicts. Using armed guards may lead to unintended consequences, such as the escalation of violence or the displacement of local communities. It is crucial to consider the long-term effects of private security operations on the stability and development of coastal communities.

Technological advancements in maritime security have also raised controversies surrounding the role of private security firms. While these firms have access to state-of-the-art equipment, there are concerns about the potential for misuse or abuse of technology. The privacy rights of seafarers and navigators may be compromised, and surveillance and tracking systems may have wider implications for global maritime security.

In conclusion, using private security firms to combat piracy has undoubtedly provided essential protection for ships navigating the dangerous waters off the coast of Somalia. However, challenges and controversies persist, ranging from legal and economic considerations to the impact on local communities and the use of advanced technology. Addressing these issues requires a balanced approach that ensures the safety of maritime operators while also considering the broader implications of private security operations in the region.

Case Studies of Successful Security Operations

One of the most pressing issues facing the maritime industry today is the threat of piracy along the coasts of Somalia. However, amidst this dark and treacherous landscape, there have been several case studies of successful security operations that have effectively combated piracy and ensured the safety of seafarers and navigators.

One such case study is the counter-piracy efforts conducted by international naval forces. Historians, diplomats, and maritime operators can learn valuable lessons from the collaborative efforts of naval forces from different countries. These operations have involved coordinated patrols, intelligence sharing, and advanced technologies to track and intercept pirate vessels. By studying these successful operations, we can gain insights into effective strategies for preventing and responding to pirate attacks.

Another important aspect to consider is the role of private security firms in protecting ships. These firms have played a crucial role in safeguarding maritime trade by providing armed guards onboard vulnerable vessels. By analyzing the methods employed by these security firms, navigators and maritime operators can better understand the best practices for securing their ships and crew.

Furthermore, it is essential to examine the economic implications of piracy on maritime trade. The impact of piracy on local communities and economies in Somalia is significant, as it disrupts vital trade routes and negatively affects regional stability. By studying successful security operations, historians and diplomats can gain a deeper understanding of the economic consequences of piracy and devise strategies to mitigate its impact.

Moreover, the psychological impact of piracy on seafarers and navigators cannot be ignored. The trauma experienced by those subjected to pirate attacks can have long-lasting effects on their mental well-being. By exploring successful security operations, researchers can identify effective support mechanisms and psychological interventions to aid those affected by piracy.

Lastly, technological advancements in maritime security against piracy have been instrumental in combating this menace. From using drones for surveillance to developing sophisticated communication systems, these advancements have significantly enhanced the effectiveness of security operations. Navigators, maritime operators, and historians can benefit from studying these technological innovations and understanding their applications in the fight against piracy.

In conclusion, the subchapter "Case Studies of Successful Security Operations" provides invaluable insights for historians, diplomats, navigators, and maritime operators. By examining successful security operations, we can learn from past experiences, develop effective strategies, and ultimately create a safer and more secure maritime environment.

# Chapter 6: Strategies for Preventing and Responding to Pirate Attacks

Risk Assessment and Planning for Ships and Crews

In "Beneath the Waves: Navigators' Nightmares and Modern Piracy Along the Coasts of Somalia," the subchapter on Risk Assessment and Planning for Ships and Crews delves into crucial aspects of maritime security in the face of piracy threats. This section of the book provides valuable insights for historians, diplomats, navigators, and maritime operators eager to understand the multifaceted challenges of piracy off the coast of Somalia.

Navigators' Nightmares: Modern Piracy Along the Coasts of Somalia

By examining the historical context and evolution of piracy in the region, this subchapter highlights the importance of understanding the root causes and motivations behind these criminal activities. Exploring the psychological impact on seafarers and navigators sheds light on their harrowing experiences and the long-lasting trauma they may face.

Counter-piracy Efforts by International Naval Forces

The subchapter also delves into the strategies international naval forces employ to combat piracy. It explores the coordination and cooperation among naval forces from various nations to ensure the safety of ships and crews. Additionally, it examines the economic implications of piracy on maritime trade and the subsequent efforts to protect global trade routes.

Legal Challenges in Prosecuting Pirates

Understanding the legal challenges surrounding the prosecution of pirates is crucial for diplomats and legal professionals. This subchapter delves into the intricacies of international law and the difficulties in securing convictions of pirates, addressing the need for enhanced legal frameworks and international cooperation.

The Role of Private Security Firms in Protecting Ships

Private security firms play a significant role in protecting ships and deterring pirate attacks. This subchapter explores their involvement, examining the benefits and challenges of employing private security personnel to safeguard maritime trade.

Impact of Piracy on Local Communities and Economies in Somalia

The subchapter sheds light on the detrimental impact of piracy on local communities and economies in Somalia. Analyzing the socio-economic consequences underscores the urgent need for comprehensive strategies that address the root causes of piracy while fostering sustainable development in the region.

Technological Advancements in Maritime Security Against Piracy

Advancements in technology have played a pivotal role in enhancing maritime security. This subchapter scrutinizes the latest technological innovations, such as satellite surveillance systems, drones, and biometric identification, that aid in preventing and responding to pirate attacks.

Strategies for Preventing and Responding to Pirate Attacks

Drawing from historical examples and contemporary approaches, this subchapter offers a comprehensive overview of effective strategies for preventing and responding to pirate attacks. It emphasizes the importance of risk assessment, intelligence sharing, and proactive planning in mitigating piracy risks.

Environmental Consequences of Piracy in Somali Waters

The subchapter delves into the environmental consequences of piracy, shedding light on how these criminal activities impact marine ecosystems, including illegal fishing and the dumping of pollutants. It underscores the interconnectedness between maritime security and environmental protection.

As historians, diplomats, navigators, and maritime operators delve into "Beneath the Waves: Navigators' Nightmares and Modern Piracy Along the Coasts of Somalia," this subchapter provides an invaluable resource for understanding the complex dynamics of risk assessment and planning for ships and crews in the face of piracy threats. Addressing the historical, legal, economic, and technological aspects equips readers with the knowledge necessary to navigate the treacherous waters off the coast of Somalia.

Best Practices in Navigation and Surveillance

Introduction:

Navigating the treacherous waters off the coasts of Somalia poses significant challenges to mariners, making it imperative for them to adopt best practices in navigation and surveillance. This subchapter aims to provide historians, diplomats, navigators, and maritime operators with a comprehensive understanding of the strategies and technologies employed to mitigate the risks associated with modern piracy.

1. Technological advancements in maritime security against piracy:

Technology advancements have revolutionized navigation and surveillance, equipping seafarers with tools to identify and deter pirate attacks. These innovations have significantly enhanced situational awareness and response capabilities, from using radar systems, automatic identification systems (AIS), and satellite imagery to deploying unmanned aerial vehicles (UAVs) and underwater drones.

2. Strategies for preventing and responding to pirate attacks:

Effective navigation and surveillance require a combination of proactive and reactive strategies. Preemptive measures such as route planning, adherence to recommended transit corridors, and practicing good seamanship play a crucial role in deterring pirates. Additionally, response strategies, including evasive maneuvers, seeking assistance from naval forces, and activating ship security protocols, can minimize the risk and impact of pirate attacks.

3. The role of private security firms in protecting ships:

Private security firms have emerged as indispensable allies in the fight against piracy. Armed security teams, embarked on vessels, act as a strong deterrent, providing an additional layer of defense. The subchapter delves into the legal and ethical implications of employing private security firms, outlining best practices for their effective deployment.

4. Psychological impact on seafarers and navigators:

Piracy incidents can profoundly affect seafarers and navigators, leading to post-traumatic stress disorder (PTSD) and other mental health issues. The subchapter highlights the importance of providing psychological support and counseling services to those affected by piracy, emphasizing the role of shipowners, employers, and relevant authorities in safeguarding the mental well-being of seafarers.

Conclusion:

The "Best Practices in Navigation and Surveillance" subchapter sheds light on the multifaceted aspects of navigating the pirate-infested waters off Somalia's coasts. By examining technological advancements, strategies for prevention and response, the role of private security firms, and the psychological impact on seafarers, this subchapter equips historians, diplomats, navigators, and maritime operators with the knowledge necessary to navigate these dangerous waters with confidence and enhance the safety of maritime operations.

Training and Preparedness of Crew Members

In the treacherous waters off the coast of Somalia, the safety and security of crew members aboard ships are paramount. The training and preparedness of these individuals play a crucial role in safeguarding vessels against the constant threat of modern piracy. This subchapter delves into the various aspects of crew training and preparedness, highlighting their significance in countering pirate attacks and ensuring safe navigation.

Crew members must be equipped with the necessary knowledge and skills to combat piracy effectively. Training programs should cover various topics, including piracy awareness, self-defense techniques, emergency response protocols, and effective communication strategies. Historically, pirates have employed cunning tactics and sophisticated weaponry, making it essential for crew members to be well-versed in counter-piracy efforts.

Furthermore, the psychological impact of piracy on seafarers and navigators cannot be overlooked. Constant exposure to threats and violence can lead to anxiety, stress, and post-traumatic stress disorder (PTSD) among crew members. Therefore, training programs should also focus on mental health support and resilience-building techniques to help individuals cope with the traumatic experiences they may encounter.

From an economic perspective, piracy has severe implications for maritime trade. Successful pirate attacks result in the loss of valuable cargo and drive up insurance costs for shipping companies. By investing in comprehensive training programs, maritime operators can reduce the vulnerability of their vessels, protect valuable assets, and mitigate financial losses associated with piracy.

While training and preparedness are paramount, it is crucial to acknowledge the legal challenges in prosecuting pirates. International naval forces, in collaboration with local authorities, should work towards establishing effective legal frameworks that facilitate the arrest, prosecution, and punishment of pirates. Crew members should be educated about the legal procedures and their rights, ensuring their actions during pirate attacks align with international laws.

Private security firms also play a pivotal role in protecting ships. By employing highly trained personnel and utilizing advanced technologies, these firms enhance the security posture of vessels. However, it is essential to strike a balance between employing private security and respecting the sovereignty of coastal states.

In conclusion, the training and preparedness of crew members are vital components in countering piracy along the coasts of Somalia. By equipping seafarers and navigators with the necessary knowledge, skills, and psychological support, maritime operators can enhance the safety and security of their vessels. Furthermore, international collaboration, legal frameworks, and the involvement of private security firms are crucial in preventing pirate attacks and ensuring the economic stability of maritime trade.

# Chapter 7: Psychological Impact on Seafarers and Navigators

Post-Traumatic Stress Disorder and Other Mental Health Challenges

In the treacherous waters off the coasts of Somalia, modern-day pirates lurk, waiting to strike unsuspecting ships and their brave navigators. The relentless attacks and constant threat of violence have left an indelible mark on the seafarers who traverse these dangerous waters. This subchapter delves into the psychological impact of piracy on navigators and seafarers, shedding light on the often overlooked mental health challenges they face.

Post-Traumatic Stress Disorder (PTSD) is a prevalent mental health condition that affects many individuals who have experienced traumatic events. Navigators and seafarers who have encountered pirate attacks are no exception. The harrowing experiences they endure, such as being held hostage, witnessing violence, or fearing for their lives, can lead to the development of PTSD. This disorder manifests in various ways, including flashbacks, nightmares, hypervigilance, and avoidant behaviors, significantly impacting their overall well-being.

Furthermore, the psychological toll of piracy extends beyond PTSD. Depression, anxiety, and other mental health challenges often accompany the traumatic experiences endured by navigators and seafarers. The isolation and confinement endured during captivity, coupled with the uncertainty of future attacks, can exacerbate these conditions, leading to a decline in mental health.

The implications of these mental health challenges are profound, affecting the individual and the maritime industry as a whole. Navigators with PTSD and related conditions may find it difficult to return to their profession, leading to a shortage of experienced personnel. The loss of skilled seafarers can disrupt global trade and hinder economic growth as maritime operators struggle to find capable replacements.

To address these mental health challenges, historians, diplomats, navigators, and maritime operators must acknowledge the psychological impact of piracy. By recognizing the unique needs of those affected, support systems can be established to provide comprehensive mental health care and counseling services specifically tailored to the maritime industry.

Moreover, preventative measures should be implemented to protect navigators and seafarers from pirate attacks. The role of private security firms in safeguarding ships and the advancements in maritime security technologies must be explored to ensure the safety and well-being of those who brave these difficult waters.

By understanding and addressing the mental health challenges navigators and seafarers face, we can create a safer and more resilient maritime industry. Through collaborative efforts, we can navigate the waves of trauma and build a future where the psychological well-being of those who sail the seas is prioritized.

Coping Mechanisms and Support Systems for Affected Individuals

In the tumultuous waters of pirate-infested Somali coasts, seafarers and navigators face harrowing challenges, both physical and psychological. The traumatic experiences endured at the hands of pirates can leave deep scars, impacting their mental well-being and ability to navigate the treacherous seas. This subchapter delves into the coping mechanisms and support systems available to these affected individuals, focusing on their unique needs and circumstances.

The road to recovery can be arduous for seafarers and navigators who have fallen victim to piracy. Post-traumatic stress disorder (PTSD) is a common consequence of such traumatic events, leading to anxiety, depression, and other mental health issues. Recognizing the importance of addressing these psychological impacts, various organizations and initiatives have been established to support affected individuals.

One such initiative is providing counseling services by maritime operators and naval forces. Recognizing the need for specialized care, these programs offer confidential and professional counseling to help seafarers and navigators process their experiences and build resilience. Support groups and peer-to-peer networks have also been established to create safe spaces for sharing experiences and fostering a sense of community.

Private security firms also play a significant role in supporting affected individuals. These firms provide armed guards on board ships to deter pirate attacks and offer a sense of security to seafarers and navigators. By mitigating the risk of piracy, private security firms contribute to the well-being of those operating in these dangerous waters.

Furthermore, international organizations and governments have implemented measures to ensure the well-being of affected individuals. This includes comprehensive medical and psychological evaluations, access to appropriate medication, and ongoing support throughout their recovery process. Diplomats and historians have further advocated including piracy survivors' stories in historical records, emphasizing the importance of acknowledging their experiences and honoring their resilience.

Coping mechanisms such as mindfulness, stress management, and self-care practices are also crucial for affected individuals. These techniques can help alleviate anxiety and provide a sense of control amidst the unpredictable nature of piracy. Navigators' nightmares along the Somali coasts have necessitated the development of specialized coping mechanisms tailored to the unique challenges faced by seafarers in this region.

Ultimately, addressing the psychological impact of piracy on seafarers and navigators requires a multi-faceted approach, combining professional counseling, peer support, security measures, and coping mechanisms. By providing comprehensive support systems, we can empower these individuals to navigate the treacherous waters with resilience and strength, ensuring their well-being amidst the ongoing battle against modern piracy along the coasts of Somalia.

Prevention and Mitigation Strategies for Psychological Impact

The psychological impact on seafarers and navigators cannot be overlooked in the treacherous waters of Somalia, where modern piracy has become an all too common occurrence. The harrowing experiences these brave individuals face can have long-lasting effects on their mental well-being. Therefore, it is crucial to develop effective prevention and mitigation strategies to address the psychological toll of piracy.

One key strategy is providing comprehensive pre-deployment training for navigators and seafarers. This training should focus on practical skills and security protocols and include psychological resilience training. By equipping individuals with coping mechanisms and stress management techniques, they will be better prepared to handle the psychological challenges they may encounter during pirate attacks.

Furthermore, it is imperative to establish robust support systems for seafarers and navigators who have experienced traumatic events. This can be achieved by creating a network of mental health professionals onboard vessels or through remote counseling services. Timely intervention and access to psychological support can significantly reduce the long-term psychological impact on individuals.

In addition to individual-level strategies, a collaboration between international naval forces, maritime operators, and private security firms is vital. By sharing best practices and lessons learned, these stakeholders can develop guidelines for preventing and responding to pirate attacks. This collaboration should also involve regular debriefings and counseling sessions for survivors of pirate attacks, fostering a sense of unity and support among affected individuals.

Moreover, engaging with local communities and economies in Somalia is essential to address the root causes of piracy. By investing in education, job creation, and economic development, we can provide alternative livelihoods for young individuals who may otherwise be drawn to piracy. This approach not only reduces the likelihood of piracy but also helps rebuild the social fabric of these communities, ultimately contributing to long-term stability.

Lastly, technological advancements in maritime security must be embraced. From improved surveillance systems to enhanced communication networks, these advancements can be crucial in deterring pirate attacks. By investing in cutting-edge technology and sharing information in real time, we can mitigate the psychological impact on seafarers by preventing piracy incidents altogether.

In conclusion, the prevention and mitigation strategies for psychological impact in the face of modern piracy must be multifaceted and collaborative. By prioritizing psychological resilience training, establishing support systems, fostering collaboration, engaging with local communities, and embracing technological advancements, we can protect the mental well-being of navigators and seafarers. Through such comprehensive efforts, we can navigate the troubled waters off the coast of Somalia with resilience and determination.

# Chapter 8: Economic Implications of Piracy on Maritime Trade

Cost of Ransom Payments and Increased Insurance Premiums

In the treacherous waters off the coasts of Somalia, modern piracy has become an all too common occurrence. Navigators and maritime operators face constant threats to their safety and the security of their vessels. As historians, diplomats, and navigators, we must understand the various aspects and implications of piracy along the coasts of Somalia. One such aspect is the significant cost of ransom payments and the subsequent impact on insurance premiums.

When a ship falls victim to pirates, the lives of the crew and the valuable cargo aboard hang in the balance. In these situations, ship owners are often left with no choice but to negotiate with the pirates and pay a hefty ransom to secure the safe release of their vessel and crew. These ransom payments can range from hundreds of thousands to millions of dollars, depending on the size and value of the ship and cargo. The cost of these payments is a tremendous burden on the maritime industry, leading to significant financial losses for ship owners and operators.

Furthermore, the payment of ransoms has a direct impact on insurance premiums. Insurers now view vessels transiting through these dangerous waters as high-risk assets, so insurance rates have skyrocketed. Ship owners must now bear the burden of excessive insurance costs, which further cripples their profitability. This increase in insurance premiums adds to the already substantial financial strain caused by piracy.

The economic implications of piracy extend beyond individual ships and companies. The escalating costs of ransom payments and insurance premiums are ultimately passed on to consumers through increased prices for goods transported by sea. This ripple effect on the global economy, as maritime trade is a vital component of international commerce.

It is essential for all stakeholders, including international naval forces, to recognize the grave economic consequences of piracy and work together to find effective solutions. By focusing on preventive measures, such as technological advancements in maritime security and strategies for preventing pirate attacks, we hope to reduce incidents' frequency and alleviate the financial burden on the maritime industry.

In conclusion, the cost of ransom payments and increased insurance premiums are significant challenges that navigators, maritime operators, and the global community must address. Understanding the economic implications of piracy is crucial for developing comprehensive strategies to combat this menace. By working together and implementing effective preventive measures, we can aim to ensure the safety of seafarers, protect maritime trade, and ultimately end the nightmares navigators face in the waters off the coasts of Somalia.

Disruption to Global Supply Chains and Trade Routes

The chapter on "Disruption to Global Supply Chains and Trade Routes" aims to shed light on the far-reaching impacts of piracy off the coasts of Somalia. This subchapter will delve into the various dimensions of this issue, examining its historical context, economic implications, legal challenges, and technological advancements in maritime security against piracy.

Piracy in the waters of Somalia has profoundly impacted global supply chains and trade routes. Historically, the region has been plagued by piracy, dating back centuries. This subchapter will provide a comprehensive overview of the history and evolution of piracy in the region, highlighting its shifting dynamics and the challenges faced by navigators throughout the ages.

The economic implications of piracy on maritime trade cannot be overstated. The financial burden on maritime operators has been significant, from increased insurance premiums to vessel rerouting. This section will explore the economic consequences of piracy, analyzing its impact on global trade and the measures governments and international organizations take to mitigate these effects.

Legal challenges in prosecuting pirates have been a major obstacle in combating piracy off the coast of Somalia. This subchapter will examine the complexities of bringing pirates to justice, including jurisdictional issues, evidentiary challenges, and the role of international cooperation in ensuring successful prosecutions.

Furthermore, the role of private security firms in protecting ships has become increasingly prominent in recent years. This subchapter will discuss the emergence of private security firms and their contributions to safeguarding vessels against pirate attacks. It will also address the ethical and legal considerations surrounding using armed security personnel on board ships.

In addition to the economic and legal aspects, it is essential to understand the psychological impact of piracy on seafarers and navigators. This section will delve into the psychological toll piracy can have on these individuals, exploring the long-term effects and available support mechanisms.

Technological advancements have played a crucial role in enhancing maritime security against piracy. This subchapter will highlight the innovative strategies and technologies developed to prevent and respond to pirate attacks. From satellite surveillance systems to advanced navigational aids, this section will showcase the cutting-edge solutions implemented to counter piracy.

Lastly, the subchapter will address the environmental consequences of piracy in Somali waters. From illegal fishing to dumping toxic waste, piracy has detrimentally impacted the marine ecosystem. This section will delve into the ecological repercussions of piracy, emphasizing the need for sustainable practices and environmental protection measures.

Overall, this subchapter aims to provide a comprehensive understanding of the disruption caused by piracy to global supply chains and trade routes. It is intended to serve as a valuable resource for historians, diplomats, navigators, and maritime operators, shedding light on the multifaceted nature of piracy and the efforts made to combat this menace.

Efforts to Safeguard Maritime Trade and Minimize Economic Losses

The maritime trade industry has long been plagued by the threat of piracy, particularly along the coasts of Somalia. For centuries, navigators have faced nightmares at the hands of pirates, causing significant economic losses and psychological impact on seafarers. However, in recent years, concerted efforts have been made to combat this menace and safeguard maritime trade.

Counter-piracy efforts by international naval forces have been crucial in deterring pirate attacks. Naval patrols, such as those conducted by the European Union Naval Force (EU NAVFOR) and Combined Maritime Forces (CMF), have significantly reduced piracy incidents. These efforts have involved joint operations, intelligence sharing, and coordinated responses to pirate attacks. The presence of international naval forces has deterred pirates and provided a sense of security to seafarers and navigators.

The psychological impact on seafarers and navigators cannot be understated. The constant fear of being attacked or held hostage by pirates takes a toll on their mental well-being. Many have post-traumatic stress disorder (PTSD) and anxiety, affecting their ability to perform their duties effectively. Efforts have been made to provide psychological support and counseling to those affected by piracy incidents, ensuring their well-being and mental health.

The economic implications of piracy on maritime trade are significant. Piracy disrupts global supply chains, increases insurance premiums, and raises the cost of goods. The estimated economic losses from piracy in Somali waters are billions of dollars. However, efforts are being made to minimize these losses. Governments, international organizations, and industry stakeholders have collaborated to enhance maritime security measures, including deploying armed guards and using technology such as satellite tracking systems and early warning systems.

Legal challenges in prosecuting pirates have been a major obstacle. Due to jurisdictional issues and the complexities of international law, many pirates have escaped prosecution. However, international cooperation has improved, leading to the successful prosecution of some pirate leaders. Efforts are ongoing to strengthen legal frameworks and hold pirates accountable for their actions.

Private security firms have also played a crucial role in protecting ships. Many shipping companies have employed private security firms to provide armed guards on board vessels transiting high-risk areas. These firms have proven effective in deterring pirate attacks and ensuring the safety of crew and cargo.

The impact of piracy on local communities and economies in Somalia cannot be ignored. Many coastal communities have relied on piracy as a source of income, leading to a cycle of violence and lawlessness. Efforts are being made to address the root causes of piracy, such as poverty and lack of economic opportunities, by promoting alternative livelihoods and development programs.

Technological advancements in maritime security have been pivotal in the fight against piracy. Innovative solutions, such as unmanned aerial vehicles (UAVs), radar systems, and biometric identification systems, have enhanced surveillance and monitoring capabilities, enabling early detection of pirate activities.

Strategies for preventing and responding to pirate attacks have evolved. Best management practices, including safe corridors, increased vigilance, and adherence to recommended security measures, have effectively reduced the success rate of pirate attacks. Additionally, establishing regional information-sharing centers and implementing anti-piracy drills have further enhanced preparedness and response capabilities.

The environmental consequences of piracy in Somali waters are significant. Illegal fishing, toxic waste dumping, and oil spills have occurred due to pirate activities. These environmental impacts threaten marine ecosystems and livelihoods dependent on coastal resources. Efforts are being made to address these issues through increased maritime surveillance and enforcement of environmental regulations.

Understanding the history and evolution of piracy in the region is crucial in developing effective strategies to combat it. By studying past incidents and analyzing trends, policymakers, historians, diplomats, navigators, and maritime operators can gain valuable insights into the motivations and tactics employed by pirates. This knowledge can inform the development of targeted counter-piracy measures.

In conclusion, efforts to safeguard maritime trade and minimize economic losses have seen significant progress in recent years. The threat of piracy along the coasts of Somalia is being effectively addressed through international cooperation, technological advancements, legal frameworks, and proactive strategies. However, continued vigilance and ongoing efforts are essential to ensure the long-term security and prosperity of the maritime trade industry.

# Chapter 9: Technological Advancements in Maritime Security Against Piracy

Surveillance Systems and Maritime Domain Awareness

Surveillance systems play a crucial role in enhancing maritime domain awareness in maritime security. The ability to effectively monitor and track vessels, identify potential threats, and respond promptly is paramount in countering modern piracy along the coasts of Somalia. This subchapter delves into the various aspects of surveillance systems and their significance in safeguarding maritime operations.

Historians, diplomats, navigators, and maritime operators will find this subchapter particularly informative, as it explores the multifaceted nature of surveillance systems and their respective interests and concerns. For historians, understanding the historical context and evolution of piracy in the region is crucial, as it provides insights into the challenges faced by navigators throughout history.

Navigators' nightmares and modern piracy along the coasts of Somalia have necessitated counter-piracy efforts by international naval forces. Surveillance systems play a pivotal role in these efforts, enabling the tracking and interception of pirate vessels and the gathering of intelligence to disrupt pirate networks. The subchapter will delve into the strategies employed by international naval forces and the technologies used to enhance their surveillance capabilities.

Additionally, the psychological impact on seafarers and navigators cannot be overlooked. The constant threat of piracy and the harrowing experiences endured by those who fall victim to attacks can have a lasting effect on individuals. Understanding the role of surveillance systems in mitigating these psychological impacts is crucial for addressing the well-being of maritime personnel.

Furthermore, the economic implications of piracy on maritime trade cannot be underestimated. Surveillance systems aid in identifying high-risk areas and enable the implementation of preventive measures to safeguard shipping routes. By providing early warning and tracking capabilities, surveillance systems contribute to reducing the financial losses incurred due to piracy.

Legal challenges in prosecuting pirates also pose significant obstacles. Surveillance systems are vital in gathering evidence and providing intelligence to support legal proceedings against pirates. This subchapter will explore the complexities surrounding the prosecution of pirates and the role of surveillance systems in overcoming these challenges.

The subchapter will also touch upon the role of private security firms in protecting ships and the impact of piracy on local communities and economies in Somalia. Technological advancements in maritime security against piracy, strategies for preventing and responding to pirate attacks, and the environmental consequences of piracy in Somali waters will also be discussed.

In conclusion, surveillance systems are indispensable for enhancing maritime domain awareness and countering modern piracy. This subchapter aims to provide a comprehensive overview of the significance of surveillance systems in maritime security, catering to the interests and concerns of historians, diplomats, navigators, and maritime operators.

Use of Drones and Unmanned Vehicles for Monitoring and Response

In recent years, drones and unmanned vehicles have revolutionized the way we approach maritime security and response efforts, particularly in the context of modern piracy along the coasts of Somalia. These technological advancements have proven invaluable tools in the fight against piracy, offering many benefits for historians, diplomats, navigators, and maritime operators alike.

One of the key advantages of using drones and unmanned vehicles for monitoring and response is their ability to gather real-time, high-resolution data from areas that are otherwise difficult to access. Historians studying the evolution of piracy in the region can now rely on these unmanned systems to provide valuable insights into pirate activities, patterns, and tactics. Diplomats and maritime operators can also use this data to formulate effective counter-piracy strategies and coordinate international naval forces in their efforts to combat piracy.

Furthermore, using drones and unmanned vehicles can also help shed light on the psychological impact of piracy on seafarers and navigators. By capturing footage of pirate attacks and their aftermaths, these unmanned systems enable researchers to understand better the emotional toll piracy takes on those who fall victim to it. This knowledge can then be utilized to develop support and counseling programs for affected individuals, ensuring their well-being and mental health.

From an economic standpoint, piracy poses a significant threat to maritime trade. Using drones and unmanned vehicles allows for monitoring shipping routes and identifying potential pirate hotspots, enabling maritime operators to take preventive measures and reroute vessels if necessary. By doing so, the economic implications of piracy on maritime trade can be mitigated, ensuring a smooth flow of goods and minimizing financial losses.

Regarding legal challenges, using drones and uncrewed vehicles can provide valuable evidence for prosecuting pirates. With their ability to capture visual and audio data, these systems can gather crucial information that can be used in court to bring pirates to justice. This technological evidence can help address the difficulties in securing witnesses and testimonies from seafarers subjected to traumatic pirate attacks.

Additionally, drones and uncrewed vehicles have played a vital role in protecting ships through the deployment of private security firms. These systems provide an extra layer of defense, allowing security personnel to monitor and respond to potential threats in real time. Integrating these technologies with private security firms has proven to be an effective deterrent against piracy, safeguarding both the vessels and their crews.

Beyond the immediate impacts on seafarers and maritime trade, piracy also has far-reaching consequences for local communities and economies in Somalia. By utilizing drones and uncrewed vehicles, we can better understand how piracy impacts these communities, their livelihoods, and their overall economic stability. This knowledge can then inform strategies and initiatives to address the root causes of piracy, promote sustainable development, and provide alternative livelihood opportunities for those affected.

Technological advancements in maritime security against piracy have also had positive environmental consequences. We can reduce the need for large naval vessels and their associated carbon emissions by utilising drones and uncrewed vehicles for monitoring and response. This shift towards more sustainable monitoring and response techniques aligns with global efforts to mitigate climate change and protect the fragile ecosystems of Somali waters.

In conclusion, using drones and uncrewed vehicles has revolutionized how we approach monitoring and response efforts in the context of modern piracy along the coasts of Somalia. These technological advancements benefit historians, diplomats, navigators, and maritime operators. They provide invaluable real-time data, shed light on the psychological impact of piracy, help mitigate economic implications, aid in prosecuting pirates, protect ships, understand the impacts on local communities, promote sustainable development, and have positive environmental consequences. As we continue to advance technologically, it is crucial to leverage these tools to their fullest extent in our ongoing efforts to combat piracy and ensure the safety and security of our seas.

Innovations in Ship Hardening and Anti-Piracy Equipment

The battle against piracy along the coasts of Somalia has been a relentless struggle, with navigators facing numerous nightmares at sea. However, in recent years, a ray of hope has emerged through the development of groundbreaking innovations in ship hardening and anti-piracy equipment. This subchapter of "Beneath the Waves: Navigators' Nightmares and Modern Piracy Along the Coasts of Somalia" explores the latest technological advancements that have revolutionized maritime security against piracy.

One of the most significant developments has been the introduction of citadels on ships. A citadel is a secure room or area on board a vessel where the crew can take shelter during a pirate attack. Equipped with reinforced walls, communication systems, and emergency supplies, citadels have proven highly effective in preventing pirates from gaining control of the ship and harming the crew. This innovation has provided navigators with a sense of security and peace of mind while navigating dangerous waters.

Another noteworthy advancement is using non-lethal deterrents to ward off pirate attacks. High-frequency acoustic devices, known as LRADs (Long Range Acoustic Devices), emit a piercing sound that disorients and incapacitates pirates, giving the crew valuable time to take evasive action. Additionally, water cannons and electric fences have been installed on ships to create physical barriers, making it extremely difficult for pirates to board vessels.

In recent years, drones have also emerged as a game-changing technology in the fight against piracy. Uncrewed aerial vehicles equipped with high-resolution cameras and thermal imaging sensors provide real-time surveillance over vast stretches of the ocean, enabling maritime operators to detect and track potential pirate vessels from a safe distance. This early warning system has proven instrumental in preventing pirate attacks and allowing naval forces to respond swiftly.

Furthermore, advancements in satellite communication and navigation systems have greatly enhanced the safety and security of ships. Real-time tracking and monitoring systems enable maritime operators to identify potential threats and reroute vessels from high-risk areas. Additionally, distress signals can be transmitted instantly to international naval forces, triggering a rapid response to any pirate activity.

The innovation and implementation of these advanced technologies have significantly improved the effectiveness of counter-piracy efforts by international naval forces. Navigators and seafarers can now operate with greater confidence, knowing they are equipped with state-of-the-art defences against piracy.

As we delve deeper into the intricate details of these innovations, historians, diplomats, navigators, and maritime operators will gain valuable insights into the evolving landscape of maritime security. By examining the impact of technological advancements, we can better understand the strategies for preventing and responding to pirate attacks, the economic implications of piracy on maritime trade, and the psychological impact on seafarers and navigators. Ultimately, these developments have protected ships and crews and contributed to stabilising local communities and economies in Somalia, paving the way for a safer and more prosperous future.

# Chapter 10: Environmental Consequences of Piracy in Somali Waters

Damage to Marine Ecosystems and Fisheries

The issue of piracy along the coasts of Somalia has far-reaching consequences beyond maritime security. One of the most significant impacts is the damage inflicted on marine ecosystems and fisheries in the region. This subchapter explores the environmental consequences of piracy in Somali waters and sheds light on the alarming implications for historians, diplomats, navigators, and maritime operators.

The seas off the coast of Somalia are rich in biodiversity, supporting a diverse array of marine life and serving as a vital source of sustenance and livelihood for local communities. However, the relentless activities of pirates have wreaked havoc on these delicate ecosystems. Piracy disrupts the natural balance of the marine environment through various means, including using explosives for ship attacks and the indiscriminate dumping of toxic waste.

Explosions caused by pirate attacks not only directly threaten ships and crew but also severely damage coral reefs and other marine habitats. These explosions can destroy vital breeding grounds, impacting the reproductive cycles of marine species and causing long-lasting damage to the ecosystem.

Additionally, pirates have been known to dispose of their waste, including oil, chemicals, and other pollutants, directly into the sea. This reckless behavior results in the contamination of marine waters, leading to the death of marine organisms and the degradation of their habitats. The consequences of such pollution extend beyond the immediate area, affecting fish populations and jeopardizing the livelihoods of local fishermen.

The decline in fish populations due to piracy has grave economic implications for local communities and the maritime industry. Fishermen who were once able to sustain their families and contribute to the local economy now struggle to find enough fish to support their livelihoods. This loss of income exacerbates Somalia's already fragile economic conditions and pushes communities further into poverty.

To address these environmental challenges, it is crucial for international naval forces, in coordination with local authorities, to prioritize the protection of marine ecosystems and fisheries. Strengthening cooperation and intelligence sharing among nations is essential in combating piracy effectively. In addition, investments in technology and surveillance systems can help detect and deter pirate activities, preventing further damage to the marine environment.

In conclusion, the damage inflicted on marine ecosystems and fisheries by piracy in Somali waters is a matter of grave concern. Historians, diplomats, navigators, and maritime operators must recognize the urgency of addressing this issue to preserve the delicate balance of the marine environment and safeguard the livelihoods of local communities. By understanding the environmental consequences of piracy, we can work towards effective strategies for preventing and responding to pirate attacks, ensuring the long-term sustainability of the region's marine ecosystems and fisheries.

Illegal Dumping of Toxic Materials by Pirates

The issue of illegal dumping of toxic materials by pirates is a topic of great concern, not only for the maritime industry but also for environmentalists and policymakers. In recent years, the waters off the coasts of Somalia have become a hotbed for modern piracy, with pirates targeting ships for ransom and engaging in illegal activities such as dumping toxic materials.

The dumping of toxic materials seriously threatens the marine ecosystem and the livelihoods of local communities in Somalia. Pirates driven by greed and disregard for environmental regulations have been known to dump hazardous waste into the ocean, including chemicals, oil, and even radioactive materials. This reckless behavior has far-reaching consequences, not only for the immediate surroundings but also for the wider region.

The environmental consequences of piracy in Somali waters are devastating. The toxic materials dumped by pirates contaminate the water, killing aquatic life, destroying coral reefs, and disrupting the ecosystem's delicate balance. This, in turn, affects the local fishing industry, a crucial income source for many communities. Additionally, dumping toxic materials poses a significant health risk to the local population, who rely on the ocean for their daily needs.

Efforts to combat this issue have been challenging due to the complex nature of maritime law and the difficulties in prosecuting pirates. International naval forces have been actively involved in counter-piracy efforts, patrolling the waters and conducting anti-piracy operations. However, the vastness of the area and the constantly evolving tactics of pirates make it difficult to eradicate the problem.

Private security firms have also played a crucial role in protecting ships from pirate attacks. These firms employ highly trained personnel and utilize advanced technology to deter pirates and prevent illegal activities. However, their presence alone is not enough to address the issue of illegal dumping. A comprehensive approach that involves cooperation between governments, international organizations, and the maritime industry is necessary to tackle this problem effectively.

In conclusion, the illegal dumping of toxic materials by pirates off the coasts of Somalia is a grave concern that requires immediate attention from historians, diplomats, navigators, maritime operators, and other relevant stakeholders. The environmental consequences, economic implications, and legal challenges associated with this issue cannot be underestimated. It is essential to develop strategies that not only prevent pirate attacks but also address the root causes of piracy and ensure the protection of the marine environment for future generations.

Efforts to Restore and Protect Somali Waters

The waters off the coast of Somalia have long been plagued by modern piracy. However, concerted efforts are underway to restore and protect these vital maritime routes. This subchapter explores the various initiatives to combat piracy and ensure seafarers' and navigators' safety in Somali waters.

Counter-piracy efforts by international naval forces have played a crucial role in curbing piracy activities. Multi-national task forces, such as the NATO-led Operation Ocean Shield and the European Union Naval Force Somalia (EUNAVFOR), have deployed warships to patrol the region and deter pirate attacks. These forces conduct regular patrols, engage in surveillance, and actively engage pirates when necessary, dismantling their operations and apprehending those responsible.

While counter-piracy efforts have primarily focused on protecting maritime trade, it is essential to recognize the psychological impact on seafarers and navigators. The constant threat of piracy has led to heightened stress and anxiety levels among those who traverse these waters. Support programs and counseling services are being implemented to address the mental health needs of affected individuals, ensuring their well-being and resilience in the face of adversity.

The economic implications of piracy on maritime trade cannot be understated. Piracy has increased insurance premiums, ship rerouting, and heightened security measures, resulting in significant financial burdens for maritime operators. Efforts are underway to mitigate these costs, including establishing secure transit corridors, using armed guards on ships, and collaborating with private security firms to enhance protection measures.

Legal challenges in prosecuting pirates have been a major hurdle in the fight against piracy. Somali waters fall under a complex jurisdictional framework, making apprehending and prosecuting pirates difficult. International cooperation and the development of specialized courts, such as the United Nations-supported Somali High Court, have been instrumental in addressing this issue and ensuring that pirates face justice.

Furthermore, the role of private security firms in protecting ships has gained prominence. These firms provide armed guards who deter pirate attacks and provide an added layer of security. However, concerns about using force and adherence to international laws and regulations persist, necessitating the development of guidelines and standards for their operations.

Piracy has had a profound impact on local communities and economies in Somalia. The hijacking of fishing vessels and disruption of maritime activities have severely affected the livelihoods of coastal communities. Efforts are being made to promote alternative economic activities and sustainable fishing practices to alleviate the dependence on piracy-related activities.

Technological advancements in maritime security have significantly enhanced the ability to detect and respond to pirate attacks. Using satellite surveillance, unmanned aerial vehicles (UAVs), and early warning systems have provided crucial intelligence and improved response times, enabling naval forces to intercept pirates before they reach their targets.

Strategies for preventing and responding to pirate attacks have evolved, incorporating lessons from past incidents. Improved coordination and information sharing between naval forces, maritime operators, and local authorities have resulted in more effective responses and increased success rates in thwarting attacks.

Environmental consequences of piracy in Somali waters are also a concern. Dumping toxic waste and illegal fishing by foreign vessels has contributed to the degradation of marine ecosystems. Efforts are underway to address these issues through increased surveillance, law enforcement, and regional cooperation.

Finally, understanding the history and evolution of piracy in the region is crucial in formulating effective long-term solutions. Historical perspectives shed light on the root causes of piracy and provide insights into the socio-political dynamics that fuel these activities.

In conclusion, restoring and protecting Somali waters requires a multi-faceted approach. Collaborative initiatives by international naval forces, support for affected seafarers, economic empowerment of local communities, technological advancements, and legal frameworks are all essential in combating piracy and ensuring the safety and security of maritime trade in the region.

Conclusion: Looking Ahead - Navigating the Future of Maritime Security

In "Beneath the Waves: Navigators' Nightmares and Modern Piracy Along the Coasts of Somalia," we have explored the multifaceted issue of piracy and its impact on various aspects of maritime security. As historians, diplomats, navigators, and maritime operators, we must understand the challenges we face and develop strategies to effectively navigate the future of maritime security.

The first significant takeaway from our exploration is the evolving nature of piracy. From its historical roots to the modern-day piracy along the coasts of Somalia, piracy has adapted to changing circumstances. As navigators, we must stay vigilant and continuously update our knowledge to avoid potential nightmares at sea.

Counter-piracy efforts by international naval forces have made significant strides in curbing piracy activities. The collaborative efforts of navies from different nations have demonstrated the importance of international cooperation in combating this global menace. However, more must be done to ensure a sustainable and long-term solution.

The psychological impact on seafarers and navigators cannot be underestimated. The trauma experienced by those who have fallen victim to pirate attacks poses a significant challenge to their well-being and performance. Addressing this issue requires the development of comprehensive support systems that prioritize the mental health of those affected.

Piracy has far-reaching economic implications on maritime trade. The disruption caused by pirate attacks and the subsequent increase in insurance premiums and security costs directly impact the global economy. Maritime operators need to find innovative ways to mitigate these economic consequences.

Legal challenges in prosecuting pirates continue to hinder efforts to bring them to justice. Cooperation between nations and establishing specialized courts can help overcome these obstacles and ensure that pirates face the consequences of their actions.

Private security firms have played a crucial role in protecting ships. As maritime operators, we must recognize their contribution while addressing the ethical concerns associated with their involvement.

Striking the right balance between security and adherence to international laws is paramount.

The impact of piracy extends beyond the realm of maritime operations. Local communities and economies in Somalia have suffered greatly due to piracy activities. It is necessary to support efforts that address the root causes of piracy and promote sustainable development in these regions.

Technological advancements in maritime security offer promising solutions in the fight against piracy. From advanced surveillance systems to improved communication technology, these innovations can enhance situational awareness and facilitate timely responses to pirate attacks.

Strategies for preventing and responding to pirate attacks must be continually reviewed and updated. By sharing best practices and lessons learned, we can develop comprehensive frameworks that address the unique challenges navigators and maritime operators face.

Finally, the environmental consequences of piracy in Somali waters cannot be ignored. The illegal dumping of toxic waste and overfishing have contributed to the deterioration of the marine ecosystem. Protecting the environment and preserving its resources must be integral to our maritime security efforts.

In conclusion, "Beneath the Waves: Navigators' Nightmares and Modern Piracy Along the Coasts of Somalia" has shed light on maritime security's complex issues. By addressing the niches of navigators' nightmares, counter-piracy efforts, psychological impact, economic implications, legal challenges, private security firms, impact on local communities, technological advancements, prevention and response strategies, and environmental consequences, we are better equipped to navigate the future of maritime security. As historians, diplomats, navigators, and maritime operators, let us work together to ensure a safer and more secure maritime environment.

www.ingramcontent.com/pod-product-compliance
Lightning Source LLC
Chambersburg PA
CBHW022108150726
47990CB00003B/1275